Do That, Do This!

Written by Liz Minister

Illustrated by Hank Morehouse

Mom's Truck
Mom's truck got stuck!

Rick and Jack
went around the back.

A rock and a brick
will do the trick.

Now Mom's truck isn't stuck.

Bad luck!

Ants in My Pants
Every day, Mr. Hill
says, "Sit still! Sit still!"
Every day, I say, "I will!
I will,
I will,
I will sit still!"

Every day, Mr. Hill says, "You've got ants in your pants!"

Goldfish

My two goldfish,
Wink and Blink—
all they do is
drink and drink.

Do you think that
they can think?

Were You Good at School Today?

What do they think I'm going to say?

Well, I got mad,
and I was bad.

When all my friends
went out to play,
I couldn't go—
I had to stay.

I made Jess fall—
I took her ball.

Then, Mr. Hill said, "You sit still! You get a book and have a look." I got some string and made a thing that went off—ping! And then I . . .

I think I'll say I was good as gold, and that I did as I was told!

Sniff, Sniff

My dog Biff
just likes to sniff—
sniff at the wall,

at the ball,

in the sand,

at my hand.

I wish he'd tell
what he can smell!

Do That, Do This!

Do that, do this!
Give me a kiss.

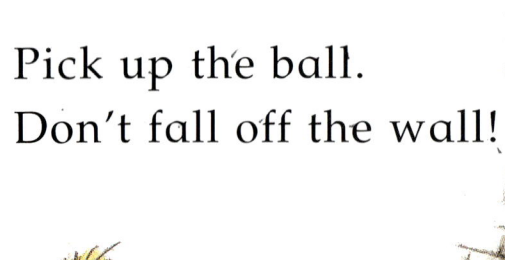

Don't make a mess
on your best red dress.

Pick up the ball.
Don't fall off the wall!

Sit still. Stand up.
Pick up your cup.

Don't spill your drink.

Don't block up the sink!

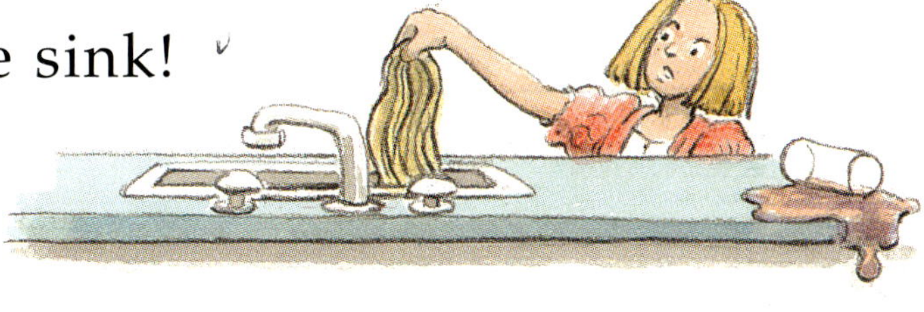

Say thanks. Don't fuss!
Be good on the bus . . .

I think I'll go to bed!